You Have the Power!
Fine Tuning Your Manuscript
Cindy Davis

You Have the Power!

Fine Tuning Your Manuscript

Cindy Davis

Cindy Davis
www.fiction-doctor.com

Cover and Interior Design by Jennifer Carson

Visit Cindy on the web at:
www.cindydavisauthor.com or
www.fiction-doctor.com

Originally published by LLDreamspell
Second edition published by: RCP

Printed in the United States of America

Introduction

Question: if an editor or critique group member suggests deleting something, do you wrack your brain for ways to leave it in? Argue your case until you turn blue? Are you so much in love with your words that when forced to delete, you save it to another file in case you want to use it in another story?

Or...

Has this scenario ever happened to you? You type, THE END, sit back and pour a glass of wine, while gazing lovingly at the computer monitor. That feeling of completion is like none other. It's like receiving a diploma, cashing a first paycheck, watching the birth of your firstborn. You pour more wine and stuff a manila envelope with the opening chapters for the first publisher on the list you've been compiling since you wrote the title on the blank page. Your hand shakes while you write, but it's fairly neat and legible so you pat on a stamp and drop the envelope in the mail slot. You do it again, and again, sending out as many submissions as your trembling fingers can produce.

It's several weeks before the first rejection letter arrives. Well, not a letter exactly—more like a bomb going off under your chair. *Dear Author, Thanks for thinking of INSERT COMPANY NAME, but we don't feel we're the agency for you...* The next day, another arrives, and then another. What's wrong with those fools, you think, this is awesome stuff. I poured my heart and soul into this. They can't *not* like it.

That's when another rejection arrives. This has to be it—the key to your future! You rip open the envelope, dropping white scraps on the floor around your feet. You yank the sheet loose, noticing it's handwritten. Yippee! I've made the big time; someone's requesting the full manuscript. You flop into a chair and read the scribbled words: *Dearest Author, Thank you for thinking of INSERT COMPANY NAME. Though your work has merit, we feel we you would benefit from the use of a professional editor.*

Ouch! You and the remaining wine retreat to the computer room to lick your wounds. Those morons. Who the heck do they think they are? I don't need an editor

You open the manuscript and sit down to read your story.

At the first paragraph you feel your eyes widening and a sense of despair gushing into your soul. The words blur on the screen.

OMG, I was sure I said the client rang the bell before going in the house. Damn, Donna's hair is blonde—when did it turn red? Oh man, the antagonist is using a Glock on page one—where did he get a .38 on page 12? No way did I type 'look' with three Os. Someone must be messing with the computer.

Hours later, you exit the room rubbing burning eyes and wearing a cloak of humility and yes, embarrassment.

Where did the run-on sentences and the mega-batch of pronouns come from? And what about all those adjectives? You were so sure you'd gotten everything. "How did I get so blind to my writing?"

It's because you're emotionally attached to it. Your brainchild, your creation. They say *love is blind*. It is.

So, how can you ferret out the problems, figure out what works and what doesn't? You've heard it before: *time* and *distance*. Every writing instructor has said this. *Time* for the emotion generated by your wonderful characters and scintillating plot to fade. *Distance* so you can view the plot with unbiased eyes.

As they said it, did you think how silly it sounded? Time and distance. Phooey. Why waste all that time? The world is missing my story. Editors can't sleep at night for waiting on this manuscript. There's an empty spot on the bookstore shelf and no other book can fill it but mine. The publishers *need* what I have. The public needs it.

Get real. Time and distance *is* needed. And humility. And a knowledge of *how* to accomplish the deed.

That's the purpose of this book, to train you to look for the bloopers, to gauge the rhythm of sentences, 'see' repeated words and an overflow of adverbs. We'll work on toning things down and tightening things up. This isn't intended to replace beta readers, just make their jobs easier.

So...put down the wine (or toss out the empty bottle) and let's get started because *You Have the Power*.

Table of Contents

Overwriting takes many forms but always results in a longer, slower moving manuscript. Overwriting buries your plot and, believe it or not, tires your reader.

Do you add every detail of the character's background—where they were born, who they first loved—because "the reader needs to know"? This is called backstory, and it's called backstory for a reason—because it belongs in the background.

If something about a character's past life forwards your plot, rather than insert paragraphs of explanation, try having the character meet up with someone from their past. A few lines of dialogue can go a long way. "Hi Joe, how're you doing?" "Great, just graduated from Princeton. Ready to start my career as an architect." Okay, the dialogue is a bit stilted, but hopefully the intention is clear. You could also show the character picking up a pad of tracing paper and a Measure Master Calculator.

A bit more about backstory—do you begin your story in the right place? Is your story a romance between Kris and Larry? Do you go through Kris's day at work, and then show her hurrying home? She sits on the train. Suddenly a man shoots into the seat beside her? This man is

Larry—and there are immediate sparks? Well, this is where your story starts. Not at work. Work is a form of backstory. The reader doesn't need to know about her work in order to appreciate and be compelled by the attraction between her and Larry.

That's one way to judge if your story begins in the right place. Does the reader *have* to know the information in order to feel compelled by your characters? It's easy to develop Kris's personality as she sits in the hard, torn seat of the train. What is she doing—reading a book or maybe briefs from work? Is she on the phone—to her best friend or her boss? A few small sentences will get the character and their personality across without pages of her work day.

Clichés. Are you a cliché-a-holic? Her skin was as white as snow. His heart beat a mile a minute. She hated him with a passion.

Use your imagination. Dig deep to find other things her skin was as white as rather than the "driven snow": Grandma's doilies, Easter lilies, Mom's bread dough.

In what other ways can his heart beat rather than "out of his chest"? How about, like a woodpecker on an electric transformer? With the reliability of a pendulum?

Is it important for the reader to know that Joe Schmoe is 7'1" and not an inch more or less? That the desert sand is 124.6° in the middle of the afternoon? Unless Joe's height or the sand temperature is pivotal to the plot line, use images and contrasts to get the ideas across instead: "Joe looked down at Michael Jordan." "The sand ate the soles of Shelly's shoes."

At the same time, it's not important to reiterate details throughout the story. Like the fact that Donna was blonde, or that Sam was elderly. Tell the reader once—or twice if it's plot related—and trust them to remember.

Do you explain in detail, the character's process of getting dressed, cooking dinner, or driving to work? Everyone gets dressed in pretty much the same way. Sits down in the same way. Unpacks groceries the same way. No need to elaborate—it's dull.

Unless Mary fell in the shower and broke her ankle, say something like: "Mary was ready for work in ten minutes; the only thing slowing her down today was a missing button on her new blouse."

Unless Roger was in an accident on the highway, just say, "Roger arrived at the office in record time." Or skip over the actions completely with a scene break.

Another way to overwrite is to just write too long.

Examples:

💣 □"The book is a treatise on living with the Indians," she told him.

It's obvious she's talking 'to him', so just use, "The book is a treatise on living with the Indians," she said. If they're the only two in the room, just say, "The book is a treatise on living with the Indians."

💣 "Calvary 1 base, looks like company en route. Counting three trucks filled with tangos. Request fast mover cover ASAP." Johnson radioed in using his flight designator for this mission, asking for fighter jets to provide air cover. *37 words*

In this example the dialogue tag repeats what the author has already said. So, just say: Johnson radioed in. "Calvary 1 base, looks like company en route. Counting three trucks filled with tangos. Request fast mover cover ASAP." *22 words*

Your writing should have two main goals: move the plot forward and delineate/develop characters.

💣 Rick accepted the paper plate Janet handed him and took a bite of the pizza. Then, he sauntered over to the counter and grabbed a beer and took a long swig, his adam's apple bobbing up and down. She watched, chewing her pizza like it was a piece of cardboard. *50 words*

This is okay but what if we tweak it a little, to shorten *and* bring the characters into better focus: Rick, adam's apple bobbing, swigged his beer. He lowered the can and belched, then accepted the pizza from Janet and perched on the next barstool. He seemed to be enjoying the cardboard-like stuff. It made her smile. *37 words*

Hopefully belching and smiling lend a more vivid picture of the people.

💣 She would jump into that tub, with the warm, sudsy water, and she would just lay there, her eyes closed, allowing her body to absorb the radiant warmth and soothing balm of those lovely bath salts. *36 words*

This can be both shortened and developed a bit more: She couldn't wait to lie back in those oil-scented bubbles and let all the office-troubles melt away. *19 words*

💣 Shell started in the living room dusting and vacuuming. From there he went to the kitchen wiping counters off, scrubbing the floor, cleaning off the table, and cleaning out the refrigerator. *31 words*

Could read: Hating every minute, Shell cleaned the entire downstairs, even the refrigerator. *11 words*

I hear you shouting, "Oh my gosh. That *blank*ing editor wants me to delete! I worked so hard to get the word count where it is." Don't worry about the word count. The story is what it is. Not all plot lines can be 70,000 words. Some stories end up at 50K. If, for some reason, you have to make a specific word count, simply add another scene. Don't pad your writing with unnecessary things. You won't fool the editor.

Let's talk about overused words: turn, laugh, look, felt, smile. Try doing a search for these words in your manuscript. I bet you're shocked at the frequency. When a character is moving around, unless your plot requires them to 'turn', just let the reader assume that's what's happening. The same with smiling. If your dialogue, or the character's actions *imply* smiling, then you don't need to *say* so.

One of my biggest peeves is the word *look* (glance, gaze, stare, etc. they're all versions of looking). Characters are always looking at something. Remember this: if you're in George's point of view, it's all done through his eyes. You're showing what's happening through his perspective. We're getting his sensations on what he tastes, sees, feels, etc. So, there is no need to *say* he looked at something. Just *show* us what he's seeing.

💣 When he opened his eyes, Seb saw a giant man looming over him. Hard ebon eyes peered down from a long face framed with a raggedy beard and long tangled hair that spilled from his helmet. If they weren't so far north, Seb might have thought he was an Ogre. Seb stared, feeling the man's monstrous hand press him down. *4 references to eyes.*

Try rewording something like this: Seb opened his eyes; a giant man loomed over him. A stern, wrinkled forehead topped a horse-like face framed with a raggedy beard and long tangled hair that spilled from his helmet. If they weren't so far north, Seb might have thought he was an Ogre. Seb tried to gulp down a lump in his throat as the man's monstrous hand pressed him down. *1 reference to eyes* but it still says the same thing.

💣 Hans saw Jackson stab at Sabrina and turned to the left as the sword cut downward, slicing off his right hand.

This should say: Jackson stabbed at Sabrina. He spun to the left as the sword cut downward, slicing off his right hand.

Ninety-percent of the time the word *that* can be eliminated without changing the meaning of the surrounding narrative. I once sent a manuscript back to an author for removal of *that* and she ended up deleting 1000 words from the overall total.

See anything wrong with the following paragraph?

Something like that. Mostly I remember the part about the horse that the Greeks snuck into Troy. In one of my strategy classes we covered the Trojan War. Not the actual war which, hmmm, my instructor said that there wasn't really any proof it happened. That there really wasn't a lot of proof about a lot of it, but that the ingenuity was real. *5 that.*

Doesn't the following read smoother?

Something like that. Mostly I remember the part about the horse the Greeks snuck into Troy. In one of my strategy classes we covered the Trojan War. Not the actual war...my instructor said there wasn't really any proof it happened, but the ingenuity was real. *1 that.*

While you go through looking for repetition, look for other words your madly typing fingers have an affinity for. *Well*, *so*, *even* and *just* are commonly overused, and are often unnecessary, but it's easy to repeat less used words also.

💣 A few sturdy tables stood in discrete locations along with a long buffet table against the far wall. Yuri stood and stretched, twisting out the kinks from the day.

Grammatically, this is right. But isn't it smoother and easier to read as: A few sturdy tables stood in discrete locations along with a ten-foot buffet table against the far wall. Yuri rose and stretched, twisting out the kinks.

💣 The power she felt flowing through her veins would not be hers for the taking. She would have had to relinquish her power to the demon. This she felt deep within her bones.

Another word that's overused—felt. Easy to slip it into a sentence because it describes what's going on inside a person. Notice above, it's used twice. But how much more visual, and more fun, to invent something like: Power, the magic with her since birth, flowed through her veins like the River Strom after a spring thaw. Use of the power would not be hers for the taking. No, nothing worthwhile ever was. Nor would it be without remuneration. She would someday have to relinquish this power to the demon. This she knew as well as she knew the sky grew dark before a storm. But for now Bree would appreciate every pulsation of energy.

Do you use redundant phrases? Things like: gathered together, sat down, shut the door behind him, climbed up. Simplify. Just use gathered, sat, shut the door, and climbed. Why? Because the verb sit *implies* downward motion. By the same token, doesn't the verb *climb* infer an upward motion? And why use 'shut the door behind him' when he's just come in the room? He wouldn't shut it in front of himself; that wouldn't make sense.

In school, when they told us to research something, we all groaned. What a chore. But research for our stories is fun. Probably because we weren't ordered to do it. Trouble is, like anything that's enjoyable, it can get out of hand.

Did you spend extreme-time learning how a machinegun works? Read tomes about the Lincoln administration? Go on a ten-hour ride-along with a policeman?

Sometimes overwriting is when you try too hard to relay what you learned. You think that since you enjoyed every aspect of the research, the reader will also. Remember this, it's important to let your newfound knowledge provide an aura for the reader rather than a detailed overload of information. Doing this takes finesse.

How much information works before the narrative bogs down? This is one aspect that will benefit by time and distance. Weeks, preferably months away from the story will often make things clear. When you return to the manuscript, you'll have new eyes and a renewed perspective. Chances are you'll be asking: who wrote this, um...stuff? (I'm having this engraved on my headstone)

Remember to give the reader credit. Trust his imagination to develop mental images so he becomes an active participant in the story. Whether his mental images are exactly what you had in your mind when you wrote the story doesn't matter. It's your job to interest the reader, to compel him to read to the end—and to buy the next book you write!

Below are some samples of overwriting and some ways to fine-tune. There is no exact right answer, but maybe you can apply the basic process to your own work.

💣 Before Sean could inquire about the caller's identity, the line went dead. He jumped up from his bed, only then noticing that there was a woman there. He couldn't remember being with anyone the night before, and wondered who she could be. He'd obviously had too much to drink—again. He turned the light off before she woke and asked him too many questions. *63 words*

The above passage has several problems. See how it could be rewritten: Before Sean could ask the caller's identity the line went dead. He jumped out of bed, only then noticing a woman's arm flung across his chest. Who was she? Damn, he'd obviously drunk too much—again. He turned off the light before she woke and asked questions. *47 words*

💣 Dina heard a car approaching from behind and walked faster, being careful to look neither right nor left. The car, almost even with her now, matched her quickened pace. She glanced from the corner of her eye at the steps leading up to the glass doors of an office building on her right, measuring the distance in her mind. *59 words*

A good visual passage, but let's tighten it a little: The rumble of an engine approached from behind. Dina walked faster. The car, almost even with her now, matched her pace. To the right, four stairs led to the glass doors of an office building. She measured the distance in her mind. *42 words*

💣 The young officer gazed at the fountain. The solid stream of water formed a protective shroud of shimmering particles around the small statue of a nude female holding a baby. His fingers twitched nervously while he anguished over his decision to accept this job three months ago. The pay was beyond anything he ever imagined, but_Grayson_never dreamed the terrible things they would force him to do. *68 words*

Could be rewritten as: The solid stream of water formed a protective shroud of shimmering particles around the statue of a nude female holding a baby. The young officer's fingers twitched. Should he have accepted the job? The money was beyond fantastic, but till then Grayson could never have dreamt the terrible things he would be forced to do. *55 words*

Another form of overwriting is referred to as author intrusion. This is where the author's voice is heard above that of the character. It's where the reader is made to know someone is telling the story.

Example: Mary knew Raymond wouldn't give in to her merely on the basis of their friendship.

This observation is from the characters' point of view; it's being told through Mary's eyes. Therefore it's not necessary to say *Mary knew* because everything in the story is what she knows, thinks, hears, etc. Simply say, Raymond wouldn't give in to her merely on the basis of their friendship.

The same here, instead of: John noticed three men standing on the opposite sidewalk, just say: Three men stood on the opposite sidewalk.

The reader should already be immersed in John's point of view, so they *know* it's what he is seeing.

💣 Linda noticed a difference in the teacher's tone. Dr. Franklin had always been somewhat excitable, especially when it came to one of his theories. When he really got wound up, he would swirl his skinny arms above that wild mop of red hair, formulating some long equation that only he could see, let alone understand. She thought that this time his voice was even more urgent, almost frantic. It was as though he sensed that if he didn't get this out, expose this knowledge he held inside, somehow it would remain hidden, forever. *93 words*

This paragraph could read: The teacher's tone had changed. Why? Sure, Dr. Franklin had always been excitable, especially regarding his theorems. Linda smiled. One time he got so wound up formulating some long equation he dropped the chalk and swirled those skinny arms above that wild mop of red hair. This time his voice was even more urgent, if that were possible. Did he sense that if he didn't expose the knowledge he held inside, somehow it would remain hidden forever? *77 words*

Another type of author intrusion is where the author foreshadows things that are going to happen. Such as: Inga sighed. Why did these things keep happening to her? She shut the door not dreaming it would be for the last time.

There's no way Inga is relating the last part since there's no way she can know the future. It jumps out of her point of view. It becomes obvious to the reader that someone else is telling the story.

It doesn't take a genius to figure that underwriting is the opposite of overwriting. Underwriting is where authors provide too little information or details and leave the reader unsure of what's going on. It leaves them without a fully developed picture of a character, or scene.

Adding emotional or physical information brings the reader into the story and lets their imagination fill in images. Adding details also expands your characters, lets the reader in on their perspective—their view of life, their surroundings, events.

Employ the five senses to provide new and unique images. The sense of sight is overused, it's easy to tell what the character is seeing, not so easy to tell what something feels, sounds or tastes like.

Try things like: The air *tasted like pennies*, tart and coppery. The monkey's fur *touched her cheek*, bringing memories of Grandfather's workshop, and the wads of used sandpaper on the floor. The air *bit into her sinuses* just like the Vicks Vapo Rub Mother used to glob on her chest.

Try this:

Go outdoors. Stand barefoot in the grass, or on your fire escape. Close your eyes and let your other senses take over. What do you hear: the rustle of daisies in the breeze? Horns honking? What do you smell: your neighbor's woodstove? Gasoline fumes? Breathe through your mouth. What does the air taste like: mildewy leaves? Tangy like acid rain? How does the grass feel between your toes: damp with dew? What does the fire escape remind you of: a bridge from which you're about to fall?

Go indoors now—wait, open your eyes first.

Now, close them again and do the same as a moment ago. What do you smell: the baby's dirty diaper in the trashcan? Do you hear the kids' footsteps upstairs? Can you tell which kid is which by the way they run? Did you get goosebumps realizing you'd forgotten the pot on the stove?

Challenge your creativity. Everyone knows how a bakery *smells*, but what does it *sound* like?

Everyone has an idea of what war *sounds* like, but what does the air *taste* like?

Take everyday things like the rumble of your neighbor's car on a cold morning. What visual image does it conjure up from your childhood: the time you went shopping with your mother and threw up on her best coat?

Your favorite bathrobe is soft on your face, but what flavorful memory does it evoke: When you and your husband went to that B&B for your fifth anniversary?

These are the sorts of images you should present to your readers; things they can sink their senses into; things that stimulate *their* memories, images. Even if it's not the exact images you had when you wrote, you've still accomplished your purpose: you've involved them in the story.

One thing to be careful of is when to add details. Certainly not in the middle of an action scene. You don't want to slow your narrative with anything. Although, your character might very well be sitting around later, recalling what happened and be invaded with all sorts of images.

Below are some samples of underwriting and examples of how to fine-tune them. As in the overwriting chapter, there is no right or wrong answer. Let the character feel, see, taste, hear, smell.

💣 She stood in the middle of the field, waiting for John to bring the briefcase. *15 words*.

This sentence provides some good images. We see a girl, alone, wondering if the person will show up. Let's try and make the scene richer.

She stood in the field, immature heads of timothy tickling her bare legs. In the distance, the tall spires of NH's Presidential Range looked like an oil painting. The breeze slipped up from behind bringing the scent of fresh-cut hay and lost loves. John's blond head should be visible on the horizon by now. He would be carrying the promised briefcase—her ticket to freedom. *64 words.*

Do you see how you impart a feel for not only the character's past, and current mood, but also her anticipation and a sense of mystery regarding the briefcase? Without jolting the reader, we've also interjected information about the season and physical location, and given an image of her upbringing (the oil painting wouldn't be thought of by a gang member or a child, etc). And...insert drum roll here...increased the word count!

💣 There wasn't a single sound in the library. *8 words*

This short sentence lends a good image. Trouble is, everyone's been in a library. We know what a quiet one sounds like. Which makes this sentence bo-ring.

What if we expand the image a bit more?

The library was like a tomb. No...more like the Callahan Tunnel at three a.m., dank and hollow and smelling like... Well, this place didn't smell like gasoline fumes, but there was a pervading aura of moldiness, and a feeling like the place might suddenly be teeming with people. Where the heck was everybody anyway? *54 words*

See here how, besides the quiet, the reader is given a sense of the character's mood, his personality, and his anticipation? At the same time, without backstory, you're aware that he's had experience in Boston in the wee hours, and you're hopefully wondering what sort of past creates this memory for him.

💣 The dirt road stretched ahead of him. As the horse moved, Matthew occasionally caught sight of the great Mississippi River glinting between the trees. *24 words.*

Again, two sentences provide good visual images. But what if it read:

Not much had changed since his last visit, except now there seemed to be more cultivation and less forest. The farmers had become more ambitious, planting a second crop of corn. A good thing, he supposed. Matt rubbed his lower back. Suddenly, a covey of quail burst from a nearby thicket. The horse lurched sideways; Matt's hand dropped to the holstered gun. Senses alert to any other sound or movement, he settled his hand on the pommel and watched the birds flutter away. Now there was just the rustle of wind through the Johnson grass and, over Mount St. Helens, a vee-shaped flock of geese heading south for the winter. *110 words*

In the rewritten example it's clear Matt has been in the saddle a long time. He shows emotion concerning the changes in his surroundings; he's alert for danger. We've interjected his geographic location so the reader can feel settled.

Who Said That?

Everyone knows dialogue is a conversation between two or more people, but what else is it?

It's a simulated conversation, not an actual transcript. It needs to be much shorter than *real* conversation and get quickly to the point. In good dialogue, characters do not speak as people do in real life; unessential words are stripped away, yet characters still sound like real people talking.

Dialogue accomplishes several tasks. It helps build characters, advance the plot, set the mood, provide humor and conflict, and make the action seem more natural—all in as few words as possible.

Dialogue delineates characters' feelings and personalities; it imparts information that would otherwise sound contrived; it provides a break from narrative.

Dialogue should *sound* real but not *be* real because if you listen to what people say to each other in real life, there's a lot of superfluous stuff that would slow your book's plot. "Hi Mary." "Hi Tim, what's new?" "Oh nothing much. Enjoying the weather?" "Yeah, it's okay." Bo-ring. Tweak it so it *seems* real. Like this: "Hi Mary, how's tricks?" "So...so. Loving the weather though!"

As above, dialogue should sound like the character, not like you. Could you remove the *he saids* and *she saids* and still know who's talking? You should be able to.

The *voices* of your characters are important. Does one squeal when she gets excited? Does another speak in a low baritone? These different voices will not only add flavor to your writing, but will also give you a method with which to differentiate when one character is speaking, rather than using funky spelling which is only confusing to the reader. More about dialect later.

Gestures are also a powerful tool. Some people drum their fingernails when they're irritated. Others crack their knuckles or "talk" with their hands. Just be sure not to overdo this. Once you've established a character's quirks, be careful not to keep repeating them. Trust the reader to "hear" those knuckles drumming each time the character opens his mouth.

All characters speak a little differently from each other. This is what's known as dialect. Their backgrounds, moods, education, etc. are reflected in their speech.

For example, how would an uneducated boy say goodbye compared to a Yale graduate? How would your grandmother ask for help with chores compared to how your mother would ask? How would your best friend bring up your bad breath compared to how your husband might mention it?

Try this exercise. Along the left margin of a sheet of paper, write some ordinary words like: bed, chair, school, car, dog, flowers, money, wallet, house, hello, medicine, telephone, restaurant, or highway. Across the top of the page, write these characters: NYC teen, Tennessee grandma, Yuppy art teacher, six year old, millennial male from London.

Draw downward lines between each character to make columns. Now, under each write a word, or words, that best describes how this person would say each word in the left-hand column. For example, the NY teen might call a house a *crib*. The Tennessee grandma might call it a home. These differences should show in your dialogue, and your narrative. The point of view character should relate the story using his specific vernacular.

Dialect provides sound and texture for the reader. But creating dialect has its drawbacks. As before, good dialogue should *sound* real, but not truly *be* real, and that's even more true for dialect.

Consider this example from Mark Twain's *Adventures of Huckleberry Finn*: "You wants to keep 'way fum de water as much as you kin, en don't run no resk, 'kase it's down in de bills dat you's gwyne to git hung."

Adventures of Huckleberry Finn is a story with great characters and plot, and if read aloud with care, it sounds authentic. But the dialect complicates and slows down the story. It makes the reader have to think about what's being said.

But, I hear you arguing: that's how the character talks. And you're right, but a balance between moving a plot and delineating the character must be developed.

How do we do that? Several ways.

1) Let the setting do some of the work for you. Is the story in the mountains of Tennessee, in a small shack in the woods, a museum in Soho, or an alley in New York City? Wherever it is, some of the discourse will be pre-set in your reader's mind.

2) People from specific areas develop mannerisms, or hand gestures, particular to their location, particular to their speech.

3) Familiarize yourself with the language of the area. Find two or three turns of speech or bits of slang. You might be surprised to find that dialect has more to do with timing and word placement than pronunciation.

Does your story have a balance between dialogue and narrative? Believe it or not, long passages of narrative tire the reader. As do page after page of dialogue. Try interrupting long bits of dialogue with character action. Maybe Tom can get up and move about the room while he's speaking, or Daisy can react to someone who's just passed by.

Now let's discuss dialogue tags. Tags are the "he saids" and "she saids' in your story. I have worked as an editor for eight houses. They all have their likes and dislikes in their books. For example, one published hated the word *was*. Did not want editors using it. Another disliked too many commas.

One thing most of them had in common was they wanted just "said" or "asked" rather than a variety of other verbs that essentially explain what the dialogue means. They also wanted active tags that *show* who's talking rather than "he said" which *tells* who is speaking.

Do you use "shouted, "cried," "groaned," etc. to make sure the reader feels the proper emotion? Or, do you insert adverbs to keep the meaning crystal clear: "said sharply," "shouted loudly" or "groaned painfully"?

Instead of *telling* the reader someone is angry or sad or hurting, make the actual dialogue *show* the emotion. Suck the reader in with your selection of words.

💣 "I want my wallet," Wanda ordered harshly.

"I want it," Jason pleaded.

"No," she said, sharply.

"If I can't carry it, I'm not going with you," Jason whined.

See how much easier this is to read:

"Give me my wallet," Wanda said.

"C'mon Wanda, I won't lose it, I promise," Jason said.

"Give it to me NOW!"

"If I can't carry it, I'm not going with you."

Let's expand the example using just action rather than tags:

Wanda put out her hand. "Give me my wallet."

Jason stepped back. "C'mon, Wanda, I won't lose it."

"Give it to me now!" She poked her fingertips in his ribs.

Jason winced but didn't relent. "If I can't carry it, I'm not going with you."

Authors have argued with me that using basically one tag—said, or asked—is repetitive. To a point, it is, but the subconscious mind is an amazing thing. After a while, the words become invisible; the eye passes over and concentrates on the actual conversation. Truly, isn't it more important to remain entrenched in the story, not the tags?

Example:

"Do you love me?" Renee asked.

"I..." Lance said.

"Do you love me?" Renee repeated.

"I. You know I..." Lance hesitated.

"I want an answer," Renee insisted.

"Damn it, you know I do," Lance shouted.

The above gets the meaning across but the tag lines are tiresome. The dialogue could be rewritten this way:

Renee put her hand on Lance's. "Do you love me?"

He looked away. Seemed to be watching something out the window.

"Lance?"

Finally his eyes found hers. "You know I—"

She squeezed his arms and he looked down his clenched hands.

"Dammit, you know I do!"

Isn't this a lot easier to read? Don't you also get a bit of a feel for the characters' personalities?

Exercise in achieving balance between narrative and dialogue. Add attributions (motion) and tags (he said/she said) to the dialogue sample below, to 1- achieve balance, and 2- make it clear three people are talking. There are no right or wrong answers.

"What's the bill come to?"

"Nothing. The sheriff said the county would take care of it. I reckon they will."

"Something else?"

"Your friend was real polite, but he kinda scared me."

"He scares a lot of people."

"But he was a real gentleman. I liked him."

"Well, you're not alone there."

"Where's the pistol?"

"I left it with Bubba. He may find a use for it."

"And you won't?"

"There's a rifle and a shotgun at the farm. That's all I'll need."

"I wonder if Mr. Farris has taken another turn in the road."

"It's possible. You look beautiful tonight."

"When will I see you again?"

"Soon as I can get away."

Make the dialogue work for you. Let it carry the emotion and the conflict. Don't be afraid to rewrite. Too often I ask authors to work on the dialogue tags and they go through and remove them without taking the opportunity to bring that dialogue into vivid meaning. Suck the reader into what's happening between your characters.

Character emotion should drive your fiction. As mentioned before, it brings characters alive for the reader. Draws them into the story. Emotionless fiction is *telling* rather than *showing* how your character feels. More on telling vs. showing later.

Let's expand a simple bit of dialogue into something bursting with emotion.

Sue was sad. *3 words*
Joe hated John. *3 words*

Yes, the reader has felt sadness or hatred, and can identify with those emotions, but feelings are more complex than that. A child anticipating a birthday might feel excited and eager, but beneath that might be worry because last year's party was a fiasco, or apprehension because last year he got educational toys instead of the bike he really wanted so he could play with his friends.

Or, a man from the mailroom receiving a promotion to management might feel anticipation for success, and excitement about the pay raise, but also trepidation for what the job entails, or fear of how the bypassed employees might react.

Let's expand on the John and Sue emotion:

Sue pulled the blanket over her head and buried her face in the pillow. *14 words*

Joe clenched his fists and held them stiff by his side. Against his better judgment, he strode away from John. *20 words*

Knowing your own character's emotions is crucial. How do they react to their own emotions? Better yet, how do you convey those reactions to the reader?

Let's take Sue and John a step further.

Prepared for a crying jag, Sue pulled the blanket over her head and buried her face in the pillow. No, dammit, she wouldn't let him do it to her again. She flung off the covers and got out of bed. *40 words*

Joe clenched his fists and held them stiff at his sides. Against his better judgment, he strode away from John. He put one hand on the doorknob. The other hand, he hammered on the raised oak panel. *36 words*

Good emotion, but let's go deeper still.

Prepared for a crying jag, Sue pulled the blanket over her head and buried her face in the pillow. No, dammit, she wouldn't let him do it to her again. She flung off the covers and got out of bed. Then she whirled around and dropped back on the comforter. No. She just couldn't compete with another woman. Again. *59 words*

Joe clenched his fists and held them stiff at his sides. Against his better judgment, he strode away from John. He put one hand on the doorknob. The other he hammered on the raised oak panel. Dammit! He turned and retraced his steps, "Joe, I'm sorry." *46 words*

See how this gives other aspects to the characters? Sue not only can feel sadness but at the same time she can feel fleeting determination and strength; she can be depressed and overwhelmed.

As for Joe: besides anger, he feels regret, remorse and, unlike a lot of people, can say he's sorry.

Also—note the increased word counts.

Are you feeling empowered yet? Ready to race to the computer and start tweaking?

No, don't leave yet.

Draw Me a Man!

We need to talk about character sketches.

One time, I asked an editing client if he did character sketches. He laughed for a long time, during which I stood frowning at the phone, not seeing the humor in my question. Finally he said, "Hell, no, I can't draw to save myself." That was the first time I received that as an answer to my question.

Usually it engenders responses like "I write by the seat of my pants," meaning they do not plan out the story or the characters before sitting down to write. I'm sorry if I hurt someone's feelings here but how shortsighted and incomplete is that?

Sure, it takes time and energy to do a sketch but to miss the opportunity to infuse all the emotion, quirkiness, thoughtfulness, antagonism, love, etc. into each and every word, action, event, or gesture...doesn't that seem imprudent? I realize it's natural to learn new things about the characters as we write. That will happen as unforeseen events unfold in that person's life.

Other authors have told me they do a sketch. It includes things like hair color, body type, favorite food, and things like that. And that's great because you can refer to it in future stories if you can't quite recall their great-grandmother's name, but there is so much more to a character than these small details. It can be difficult to keep track of details, especially if you have a number of pivotal characters. And it's these details that can lead to the conflict that's so essential to the writing of today's fiction.

One thing I've found helpful in learning to know your characters is to interview them. Imagine you're sitting together over a cup of coffee. Ask them hard questions and write down their answers in the first person, as if they are answering you directly. A cool result I've found to this exercise is that you often end up using some of those responses in the story!

Ask hard questions that make your character think. For example:

What is your most painful memory?

Your most embarrassing moment?

The secret you've never told anyone?

The thing that makes you angriest?

The thing that made you cry the hardest?

Your greatest disappointment?

Your greatest disappointment about the person nearest to you?

The moment you felt the most crushed?

Your own least favorite physical feature?

Your first memory?

What is in your refrigerator, top desk drawer, bathroom trashcan?

The sketch should be as detailed as you can make it. You should have one on most every character. Even minor ones. Some of the information will end up in the story. Interesting, different, conflicting, idiosyncratic, etc., people help beef up your dialogue *and* the plot.

A character sketch should contain all of the things below. It will, undoubtedly, cover several pages. Go into detail. Have fun.

physical characteristics

quirks

favorite things:

sports teams, musical groups, radio stations, places to shop, cars he's owned, cars he covets,

least favorite things:

sports teams, musical groups, neighbors, dog breeds

where he was born,

where did he go to school (did he do well in school? get along with peers, teachers, etc)?

upbringing and that of his parents

were there siblings? What was their relationship with character and each other?

what does he do in his spare time? sports? tv? Music, play instruments...

what is in his refrigerator?

what is in his trash?

what is in his school locker?

does he gamble, play/watch sports, movies, attend plays, addicted to video games, etc.

music he likes

does he take part in events in town/city or just go to watch, or not go at all

male friends

female friends

smoke, drugs, drink

quirks--any habits whether unusual or common

career choice--why did he choose this career, or, has he decided on a career?

higher education

sexual relationships/marital status/relationships with neighbors

where does he live? Why? what kind of car does he drive?

political affiliation

is his bank account current? VISA paid?

In 2003, in an otherwise positive review of *Harry Potter and the Order of the Phoenix,* Stephen King observed that JK Rowling "never met [an adverb] she didn't like. Harry," King noted, "speaks quietly, automatically, nervously, slowly, and often—given his current case of raving adolescence—ANGRILY."

What is an adverb? By definition it is the part of speech that modifies a verb, adjective, or another adverb. Adverbs answer the questions when, where, and how. Many adverbs end in LY: quickly, slowly, sadly, happily. Others can be just as overused: now, that, just, soon, also, too, even, very, about, strange, beautiful, handsome, tall, short, big, little. Which makes them easy to identify.

It's easy to dump adverbs into your narrative. Everyone knows happiness, quickness, sadness. It's easy to rely on adverbs to do the work. You might be surprised how many you use. Open the Find feature of your writing program. Then type in LY and a space, then hit Enter. How many did you find? What comes up isn't all adverbs but you can scroll through and see what's what. Surprised?

Your writing will be stronger if you work at eliminating adverbs. Substitute strong action verbs or physical movement that creates visual images. It's easier than you think.

Don't write that someone clenched his teeth *tightly*, there is no other way to clench teeth.

Don't say she went quickly. Say she *ran* or *sprinted* or *hurried*.

Don't say she spoke softly. Say she *murmured* or *whispered*.

These are easy enough, and pretty self-explanatory. But let's try something that requires more thought.

💣 Mary prodded gingerly at the remains of what had once been a chicken leg, wishing she had the nerve to feign a headache, anything to avoid actually eating the charred meat. *2 adverbs*

How about this instead:

Mary poked the burnt remains with her fork. It used to be a chicken leg. No way anyone could tell now. Where was the inevitable headache that reared up during one of these get-togethers? Dare she fake one? Anything so she wouldn't have to eat the charred meat. *Zero adverbs*

💣 Sheila was clearly enjoying Ann's distress. "After all," she said, "I could hardly strike him for thinking almost exactly the same thing I was, could I?" *3 adverbs*

Try instead: Ann frowned, which made Mary giggle. "After all," she said. "It was obvious he was thinking the same thing. What was I supposed to do, strike him for it?" *Zero adverbs*

This goes along with the previous chapter regarding how to make the dialogue *sound* real without actually *being* real.

💣 George finally got up the courage to carefully walk into his boss's office. *2 adverbs*

Instead: George swiped sweaty palms on his thighs, then pushed open his boss's office door. *Zero adverbs*

Using a body action such as sweaty hands *shows* George's bolstering himself. Also, instead of carefully walking, note that he pushes the door open. This shows the reader he's gained some courage. Or you could use a milder verb, like *eased* to show him opening the door a bit more hesitantly. Either way, the action gives the reader a visual image—a man preparing for a confrontation.

💣 Doreen walked silently through the pitch black of the deserted, empty house, fingers pushing lightly on each closed door.

Instead: Doreen crept through the blackness of the deserted house, fingertips pressing on each closed door.

💣* The woman walked sexily across the living room.

Instead: The woman sashayed across the living room, hips swaying like a pendulum, breasts thrust against the silky fabric of her blouse.

Though not everyone will agree that the way she walks is sexy—smile—you would agree that there's more visuality in the second example, right?

Adverbs are a useful and necessary form of speech and there are times when no other word or combination of words will suffice. But the general rule is: don't use adverbs till you've exhausted other possibilities.

The word pronoun is taken from the old French, "pronomine." Literally translated, it means *instead of a noun*. He, she, it, they, you, this, that, which, who, are pronouns.

Many authors begin a paragraph with the character's name, then follow with a whole page of *she* and *her*.

Too many pronouns are distracting. They overshadow your subject and blur the focus of your scene. On top of that, they are repetitive. You wouldn't want to read a paragraph with the word *dog* repeated ten times, would you?

Eliminating pronouns is tough. It often requires sentence restructuring but, like the elimination of adverbs, the final result is a tighter more compelling narrative.

💣 Living in Newport Beach was another goal she had already achieved. She loved the beach and had always wanted to live there. She lived right on the peninsula where all the action took place. *3 pronouns*

Could say: Living on the beach was just another dream Maria had achieved. Parties, expensive shops, high profile people, she loved them all, right down to the bicycle cops wearing shorts that exposed well muscled calves and taut thighs... *1 pronoun*

You see, we've achieved the same objective: showing Maria's love of the beach, but also incorporated some of her personality in regards to the beach itself. *And*...eliminated two pronouns at the same time.

💣 Brenda drew in a long, deep breath and let it out in a slow hiss. Then, the memory of the day she received the job offer came to her mind and a hint of a smile crossed her face. She'd been in a terrible mood after engaging in verbal combat with her new publisher. *5 pronouns*

Could say: Brenda drew in a long, deep breath and let it out in a slow hiss. The memory of the job offer brought a smile that widened at the thought of the new publisher's face, handsome with a hint of a quirkiness that wasn't showing today. The smile died at the thought of the verbal combat he'd initiated. *1 pronoun*

Here again, we've eliminated pronouns but also developed a bit of Brenda's character in her opinion of the new boss and the fact that he'd instigated the confrontation between them.

💣 That was the question of the day, Lana thought, since he was out of town the day she interviewed with John Richards. Just then, the door flew open. Lana jumped so high she swore she floated above the sofa for a split second. A man in an expensive suit strode toward her and she heard her heart thumping. His eyes washed over her and his brows raised in recognition. *10 pronouns*

Could say: That was the question of the day, since he was out of town during the interview with John Richards. Just then, the door flew open. Lana jumped so high she envisioned dangling over the sofa like a wind-chime. A gorgeous man wearing an expensive suit strode across the carpet and her heart hammered in reaction. His glance showed appreciation. His brows raised in recognition. *5 pronouns*

Here, we've done away with some *telling* (more about showing vs. telling later), cut the adverb count in half, eliminated 5 pronouns, replaced a too-common image (heart thumping) with (hammered), and added a simile (like a wind-chime).

💣 Fred fought to stay awake by widening his eyes and staring directly at his computer screen. He tried to muster enough energy to actually work, but he lost the struggle with himself. His vision blurred, and became a grainy cloud on Mount Snow. He caught the shadow of himself shushing down the trail. He leaned left. He leaned right. Just as he was about to cross the finish line, he saw red out the corner of his eye.

The streak of color passed him and he groaned in dismay. *15 pronouns*

Could read: Fred fought to stay awake by bending forward and staring at the computer screen. Deadlines loomed tomorrow, the boss would be waiting at the office door, palm out. But damn, it was no use trying to work; two nights without sleep had taken their toll. His vision blurred—to a grainy cloud on Mount Snow, the sun climbing along the far ridge. Suddenly he was shushing down the trail, pushing up clouds of freshly fallen powder. He leaned left, feeling the stretch of calf muscles; a slight movement to the right brought up a new snow-cloud and a blast of frigid air into his lungs. He bent at the waist and, just as he was about to cross the finish line, a flash of red whizzed past, leaning into the blue strip of tape a millisecond ahead. *5 pronouns*

Fine tuning takes time and work, but makes the overall reading more of a pleasure, more compelling, more active. You can do it. You have the power.

Woulda Shoulda Coulda

In sentences written in active voice, the subject of the sentence is performing the action expressed on a second subject. The boy chose the girl. Subject=boy, verb=chose, second subject=girl. Passive voice is the reverse: The girl was chosen by the boy.

In active voice, the action is up front. It moves the story. In passive voice, the subject takes background to the second subject. Confusing when explained that way. Let's just say: passive voice slows action—puts it out of focus.

Passiveness is frequently portrayed by sentences using the verb 'to be' (was, had, were, had been, would have been) in conjunction with another verb. Example: would walk, were loving, had punched, was talking.

Was is the most overused, probably because it's the way we talk. *I was going with John. I was going to do it later.* Sorry, that's not right. I should've said: *I was gonna do it later.*

Another passive form I'm coming across more and more often is 'started to' and 'began'. Remember that if you 'start' or 'begin' to do something, it infers you're going to stop—be interrupted. Which isn't the case. Usually the action is going to continue through to its completion, which means 'start' and 'begin' become moot. So...instead of 'started to dial', just say 'dialed'. Instead of 'began to run', just say 'ran'.

It's simple to fix passive voice by replacing with action verbs.

💣 The plane she was on was going four or five hundred miles an hour.

Could read: Her plane scorched through the clouds at five hundred miles an hour.

💣 Jenny sat in the high chair and started swinging her feet annoyingly.

Could say: Jenny sat in the high chair kicking her feet. Thud thud went the tiny shoes against the footrest. Thud thud thud.

💣 Deja vu, was what Leif thought—not only because, for the second time that month, right before his eyes, someone was being hauled out of a room in a body bag but also because he and the office busybody, were standing off to the side in a very sneaky sort of way at the scene of the crime.

Could say: Déjà vu. For the second time that month, right before Leif's eyes—he slammed them shut, counted to three and then opened them again—damn, still there. Unbelievable, the second time in a month they hauled somebody out in a body bag. And...for the second time, he and the office busybody hid off to the side of the crime scene.

💣 The professor could hear the footsteps of hard-soled shoes in the hall.

Could say: The professor heard the clip clop of hard-soled shoes approaching in the hall. Or, better still: The clip clop of hard-soled shoes approached in the hall.

💣 Wanda's first memories were of a small, two-bedroom trailer in Atlanta, Georgia, where her life was begun.

Could say: Wanda leaned back in the lounge chair recalling the old trailer in Atlanta, Georgia where she grew up.

💣 Laura was an exceptionally pretty child. She had emerald green eyes with had gold-specked centers. Her face lit up when she smiled; dimples decorated the corners of her mouth. Her blonde hair curled around her face in bouncing ringlets tied up with red ribbons. Laura wore old clothes given her by relatives, or ones purchased at garage sales.

Could say: Laura was a happy child with emerald eyes and blonde curls. Although the family struggled to survive on her father's scholarships, she didn't mind the hand-me-down clothes.

●* Richard had come back from the war a changed man. The easy-going teen with a penchant for redheads had vanished. After the war, he had only met with us a couple of times...and even then he had had very little to say. He had grabbed a bottle and retreated to a little shack back in the woods of northern Vermont. I had tried to stay in touch with him, but there was no effort to maintain the friendship. Years later when he had approached me with his "proposition," I had refused as much from pity as from anger. It had been a squalid little attempt at blackmail, and I wasn't impressed. I wrote it off as him being drunk.

Could say: Richard returned from the war a changed man. The easygoing teen with a penchant for redheads had vanished. We got together a couple of times over the years...but even then he spoke very little. Apparently the abounding rumors...that he took whiskey as a roommate at that little shack in the woods of northern Vermont were true. I tried to stay in touch, but received no likewise effort to maintain the friendship and eventually gave up. Years later when he approached with his "proposition," I refused as much from pity as anger. His squalid, unimpressive attempt at blackmail got written off as a drunk's ramblings.

Not all sentences that contain a form of the verb *to be* are in passive voice. For example, the sentence "I am holding a puppy" is active, but it uses the verb *am*, which is a form of *to be*. The passive form of that sentence is "The puppy is being held by me."

Compound sentences, two sentences/thoughts joined by *and* or *but*. They are good if used in moderation. Be careful not to overuse. As you read through your story, preferably out loud, you should be able to hear them. Remember that the second half of that compound sentence is diluted by the distance. Essentially it becomes passive.

💣 "I mean to the east," Gad said. "I hear there is a kingdom that lies beyond the Ten Mountains, beyond the stronghold of the Glenfriars, and further than that, on the other side of the world, there's the Land of Tree and Hill. Men are tall there, like giants, and women are slender and graceful. They live on mountains, higher than the eye can see, a thousand cities in caves and hidden glens. They ride lizards larger than horses, with golden scales."

Could read:

"I mean to the east. I hear there is a kingdom that lies beyond the Ten Mountains, beyond the stronghold of the Glenfriars." Gad scratched his head. "Further than that, on the other side of the world, there's the Land of Tree and Hill. Men stand tall there, like giants. The women are slender and graceful. They live on mountains higher than the eye can see, a thousand cities in caves and hidden glens. They ride lizards larger than horses, with golden scales."

💣 My father stared in shock and my brother had a grin on his face from ear to ear that made me even angrier. I slammed the door behind me and stampeded toward the garden. But as I got there, I slowed my pace and took a deep breath and let the adrenaline rush through my body. I was half in shock and half amused when I pictured my father's face. I hadn't lost my temper like that in a long time and I was surprised at how good it felt.

Try this version:

My father stared in shock. My brother wore a grin from ear to ear that made me even angrier. I slammed the door behind me and stampeded toward the garden.

But as I got there, I slowed my pace, took a deep breath to let the adrenaline rush through my body. I was half in shock and half amused when I pictured my father's face. I hadn't lost my temper like that in a long time. It sure felt good.

Another way to 'write passive' is by using

filter words. Filter words take the reader slightly out of the point of view. They slow the forward motion of the plot.

Filter words are ones such as: I saw, she knew, he heard.

When writing in a specific point of view you are giving the perspective of that character, relating things they personally are seeing, hearing, tasting, touching, etc., so therefore all you need to do is SHOW what that persona is seeing, hearing, etc. rather than TELL about it.

Think about yourself: when you hear a dog bark, do you think *I just heard a dog bark*? No, you simply *hear* the dog. In that manner, so should your point of view character hear the dog.

Example: Looking up and trying to forget about the most recent among the countless times I misheard something, I SAW Carla, my freshman field hockey teammate.

You might reword something like this: I couldn't even write down the countless times I misheard something. Nothing new there. Behind me, about half the football field behind me was Carla, my freshman field hockey teammate.

Notice how we are witnessing Carla's approach without being TOLD.

Another example: I KNEW she'd always be a second or third stringer, but I liked having her around.

Try wording something like this: She'd always be a second or third stringer, but I liked having her around.

Another example: The front door opened and closed, and LILA COULD HEAR the floorboards creaking under his weight.

Try something like this: The front door opened and closed, the hallway floorboards creaked under his weight. Goosebumps stood at attention on Lila's arms.

Remember though, passive voice exists for a reason. It is particularly useful in three situations: 1- when it's more important to draw the reader's attention to the person being acted upon. (The boy was apparently chosen by the girl.) 2- when the person being acted upon is not important. (The boy was observed being chosen by the girl.) 3- when we don't know who's performing the action. (The boy was chosen.)

Yikes, enough of the school lesson!

You Tell Me Yours, I'll Show You Mine

Telling vs. showing is one of the most difficult concepts for authors to grasp. Showing a scene is a way of bringing the reader into the story. A way of letting them experience things up front and personal, through mental pictures, sensory images, emotional connections. As if the event is occurring as you're reading the story—even if it's written in past tense.

Telling is a form of author intrusion, where the author tries to make the reader *see* things his way. Why is there so much emphasis on showing instead of telling? Showing emphasizes the character's reaction to something rather than the author's description of it. It immerses the reader in images, senses, and dialogue rather than explanations. Third, it presents images in ways readers may not have seen or felt before.

The question is, how to go about doing this? One way is to use metaphors and analogies to compare the way things look, smell, sound or taste to that specific character. I stress—to that specific character. The point of view character.

Rather than *tell* the ocean breeze smelled like salt, *show* how the smell reminded the character of a romantic date he once had. Or how the breeze tickled his nostrils. Or had him watching another beachgoer's reaction to the same scent.

Let the sounds, sights, smells, etc. of your setting's everyday life permeate the scenes. The way a character reacts or thinks about the things around him deepens the scene, develops the character. *Shows* the reader.

💣❊□The man's movements had been deliberate and slow, which seemed to go with his long and extremely lank form.

This is pretty descriptive, paints a good enough picture. But try this:

He removed the container from the fire and placed it by the worn bedroll, his thin arms and legs moving as if on rusty hinges.

Better picture, right?

💣❊ Sonja decided to turn down the flame and put her romantic ideas on the back burner.

Though the example raises questions and compels the reader to read on, what about this:

Sonja sighed and pushed back the chair. Seemed like heroes only came along in fiction stories. Never in real life. Maybe it would be better not to write any more, it only made her sad. Then again, the way that biker's thigh muscles rippled...

Always be thinking how the point of view character sees what's going on. Rather than saying, Debbie sat on the bed, show it creaking under her weight, or its legs scratching across the bare wood floor. The creak or scratch should portray *how* she sat on the bed. If she's angry and throws herself there, it'll be more likely the legs will scrape and the bed will bang against the wall. Conversely, if she's calm, she might drop on the bed and it won't make any noise, but might puff up the scent of fabric softener from the quilt.

💣 The city suffered significant damage in the blast.

The example creates vivid memories the reader recalls from past news stories. But what if we expand it?

Among the ruins, the reflection of the sun on the shards of glass on the road was so strong Joe had difficulty keeping his eyes open. Today, the smell of death had eased a little, but where houses collapsed into tile-covered heaps stank like…well, he didn't want to imagine an vision to go with that. Great swarms of flies lifted then resettled as he passed.

💣 Marion woke with a scream upon her lips. She was gasping for air and her whole body felt as though it were on fire.

Nightmares commonly wake people. Though it's a familiar sensation to all readers, few authors do it right. That space between sleeping, dreaming and waking plays with the POV. How much of a dream, after all, are we aware of? How much of it can we put into words? Also, after a while, like any repeated image, even a nightmare can lose its power to influence. Sometimes skipping over it can be just as effective.

Try something like:

Marion sat up in the bed scrubbing the latest nightmare from her mind. Many things on the agenda today: dentist, job interview, parent-teacher conference, grocery shopping. For the first time, she welcomed a busy schedule. It would help keep her from dwelling on the reasons for the nightmares—the relentless string of anonymous letters.

Never be satisfied. Always strive to make things more emotional, more active, more conflicting, more compelling.

Strong, determined characters are what readers remember. Rhett Butler, Nancy Drew, Tiny Tim. These characters possess qualities that keep you awake, make you think, bring back memories. They seem alive.

Strong characters talk and act within their personality—that is predictably—until pushed beyond their limits. Pushing characters beyond the norm, showing what they're really made of, is what makes good fiction. How many times have you been surprised when the character did something totally unexpected? Even if you didn't agree with what they did, wasn't it compelling? Didn't it make you want to read on? Did you talk to your friends about them?

What does your main character think about herself as a person? How does that compare to the way her lover sees her? If she thinks of herself as a go-getter, someone who's confident and secure, he might see someone willing to kill for a promotion.

Do any of us see ourselves as weak or impatient? It's easy to see it in others though, isn't it?

Has anyone ever told you exactly what they think of you? After you got over the *mad* and thought about what they said, how did that opinion differ from one you've had about yourself all these years?

Keeping that in mind: what does your character think about other characters? Not the way they look, but the way they are as people. We all form mental opinions about people we meet. First impressions, they say, are lasting. These first impressions in your fiction are good. They develop not only the point of view character, but also the person he/she is meeting. It doesn't matter if this impression turns out to be wrong; it portrays the character as human, fallible. After all, our first impressions aren't always right, are they?

In later stages of the story, does the character view these persons in the same way? Or have circumstances changed this perspective? Plot events change characters, sometimes for the better, sometimes not. Those same plot events also reformulate our opinions, make us see things differently.

The same goes for your setting. It can change a person's perspective. For example, if your character is mugged on a particular street corner, won't her perspective of that street be affected forever? Mightn't she even avoid walking there?

Or hold her handbag closer? Dart her eyes around nervously?

These types of evaluations deepen your character, and also allow the reader to form mental impressions of characters, events, or settings.

Here is a bit of character self-evaluation:

Laura beamed her million-dollar smile at Jim. She knew some in Hollywood laughed at her now and again because of her down home "awe shucks" wide-eyed approach to life. She wasn't about to change to fit in. If anyone from her hometown remembered her it certainly wasn't as the successful actress she was now. As a kid she'd been scrawny with buckteeth that looked even bigger because of the too-tight French braids her mother wove daily into her blonde hair.

See how Laura's opinion contrasts with the antagonist's view of her:

Sean found himself eyeball to breasts with the most gorgeous woman he'd ever laid eyes on. The blonde haired goddess towered over him by a good six inches making her almost six feet tall. A virtual Amazon. Her silk blouse was the exact shade of green as her eyes. Her expression was one of mild amusement. What was so funny? He clamped his fists tight. Well, she wasn't the first to laugh at his height.

A stereotypical character is one that's been etched in the reader's mind. A dirty homeless person. A well-dressed businessman. A serious, shushing librarian.

Try taking your characters beyond this accepted image; give them traits that are unique to them as people and unexpected by the reader. A prim and proper, clean homeless person. A businessman wearing wrinkled slacks. A librarian who tells jokes in a voice an octave above a whisper.

Settings can also be stereotypical. A thunderstorm is known to instill suspense. A crowded subway fosters insecurity. A field of clover inspires happiness.

But can you go further? *Use* that setting, and the image it produces for the reader. If, in that field of clover, Joe is attacked by a wolf, won't fields of clover produce an entirely new image for him after that? Or maybe he carries a gun whenever he's out walking. What if, during the worst thunderstorm of the year, Carl asks Jeannie to marry him? Will she be a bit nostalgic during subsequent storms?

In the above examples, the characters' frames of mind are forever changed. And will keep changing as the story unfolds. Every plot situation alters the character's disposition and humor.

Here's an example of a character's mood:

The oversized wall clock behind the nurse's station read eight-thirty. Clara kicked the blood spattered white shoes from her aching feet. She should have been out of here an hour ago. Her shift ended at seven-thirty but as usual disaster struck at the stroke of seven and here she was preparing to trudge home *late* and microwave another lonely TV dinner.

See how it changes just a few pages later:

Clara tilted her head thoughtfully at the letter of promotion. Here was the opportunity for an entirely new life she had been begging for just hours before. Was she ready for it? Yes, most definitely.

Another example of a character's mood:

Donna Branch's fingers pummeled the tissue to shreds. If he thought she'd kowtow like a geisha—anything you say, Daddy, since it's for the company, Daddy—then, he had another think coming; she was his daughter dammit, not a chess piece he could move at his merest whim.

And an excerpt from a few pages later after she learns her father's got kidney disease:

Donna felt like the floor had buckled underneath her. As much as she'd battled with him all her life, she never considered the idea that he wasn't immortal. That someday he might actually be gone from her life.

What are your character's strong points? Weak points? These should be outlined in detail in your character sketch, which I hope you do on every character.

Does she have a specific goal, and a strong aim toward this goal throughout the book? Is this the only thing she wants throughout? Hopefully not. As above, goals and reactions should change throughout the story.

If she wants something else, are the two things conflicting at all? There should be places in the manuscript where your character worries how she can achieve everything she wants. And at what price? Developing this inner struggle creates depth of character. She should grow and change through the story, learn something by the experience.

Do your characters have more than one function in the story? Example: Does the crabby next door neighbor double as Cub Scout leader? Is the pharmacist also a ballroom dancer? Is the hotel maid also the main character's sister-in-law?

Try this exercise. On the left side of a sheet of paper, make a list of your characters. On the right, note their role in the story. Can you combine any of the roles? This *combining* can create new and greater conflicts and provide possibilities for sub-plots or twists to the original plot.

How, you ask? What if that hotel maid/sister-in-law is the main character's lover—or his murderer? The plotline you created for her at the outset would expand and/or change completely. Think of all the new conflicts that could come from this change.

Blending characters has another positive result, it decreases the total number of characters for the reader to remember—hones the geography of the story.

Your character has motives for things they do, even if he simply decides not to answer the phone, or get out of bed in the morning, these motives must make sense. You cannot—must not—have the character to do something simply because you like the scene. Or, as one author once told me, "I spent days writing that scene, I don't want to throw it away." The character's actions must forward your plot in a logical way. Be willing to rewrite or delete a scene, or—heaven forbid—a chapter. Your story will be stronger for it.

Are you able to inflict injury on your characters? I ask this frequently at workshops and often receive wistful smiles and head shakes. You created and molded your people. They are part of you. If your characters worry, cry, or ail, it's a pain you experience also. It keeps you up at night.

Which makes me ask: are you striving to produce perfection, a character who doesn't fear, doesn't care, doesn't know the emotion of loss? As has happened through history with Rhett Butler, Nancy Drew, and Tiny Tim, don't you want your readers on the edge of their seats worrying, biting their nails as they fear for the characters' safety? Then you have to let go. Take chances. Inflict wounds. What's the say? "Kill your darlings"!

You have the power. You know what to do.

Et Tu, Brute?

Where did your protagonist go to elementary school?

Which bully hung him from a hook in the locker room when he was twelve? Was that his most embarrassing moment?

Who did he vote for in the last election? Chances are, you don't know. When I ask authors questions such as these, more often than not, the answer is, "What difference does it make?"

Well, if you don't know the answers to those questions, and dozens more, you don't know your character well enough. He won't be as alive on the page as he might be. It's crucial to spend as much time developing your antagonist as your protagonist. There's a ninety-nine percent chance these events won't end up in your book, but they will be in the back of your mind, they will form the way he talks, the emotion he either releases or holds inside.

Does your antagonist have a chance to tell his side of things? How many times have you, after hearing the bad guy's story, wished for him to win over the adversity, to escape authorities? That's because the author did a great job of presenting the antagonist's viewpoint. How to do this though without resorting to the dreaded backstory and long sections of narrative?

If the story's told from the point of view of the main character—the protagonist—you must somehow show the antagonist's story through outside events, dialogue, or at most, a confession. If he is lucky enough to have his own point of view, the story will unfold easily. Don't though, present passages of backstory. Let his truth come out in bits and pieces as the story unfolds. Give glimpses of things that made him feel the way he does. Give the reader a new outlook on the situation each time. You'll help develop sympathy for him.

Does the antagonist have what she considers a logical motive for doing what she did? If she's sane, and simply driven over the edge by circumstances beyond her control, the reader will empathize with her, maybe even root for her to succeed in her quest.

Does your antagonist have times when he wants to quit running, or stealing, or murdering? Try and show his change of mood or attitude in the story. Maybe he picks up the phone to turn himself in. Maybe she writes in a journal. Maybe she broods at her desk.

Is there a place he likes to go? What's special about this setting? Does he value the secrecy of it? How does his mood change when he's there? The questions that opened the chapter—can you answer them for the antagonist? You'd better be able to.

Something I've found helpful is to write a few pages detailing the antagonist's problem—a sort of character sketch. If it's a crime story, you might want to write a detailed outline of the crime in first person, as though it's his personal diary entry (Today I went shopping. I murdered the paperboy on the way home. He refuses to leave the paper on the porch).

Detailing the events really helps put your character in perspective. In the case of a crime novel, also delineates a timeline of events, which you can refer to as the story unfolds.

If you involve your antagonist as a real person, the reader will follow your story with energy. Isn't that what you want?

In the next example, the teenage character is determined to go to another planet to attend school. Her father remains adamant throughout the story that she cannot go, that she belongs where she is—on the family farm.

The reader's left to dislike the man until three quarters through the story when he's speaking to a comatose friend about the situation: "I don't know, Seli," Will said, watching the monitor blip a zigzag line. "I often wonder if I'm doing the right thing with Marta. She seems so earnest in her desire to attend that academy." He shook his head. "I know nothing of outer space and schools. I only know of farming." He studied his thick hands clasped on the edge of the bed.

"With these hands I can work the land; I can plant and harvest enough food to feed half of Agoral. I can break a wild equine and make it tame."

He let his hands fall limply into his lap and made a point to look away from them. "Yet I cannot seem to hold onto my daughter." He gazed at Seli with sad eyes, eyes that contained tears. "I couldn't bear to lose another of my children."

Don't you have a different opinion of him now? This is what you must strive to achieve.

Roll 'Em!

Maintaining a story's forward motion for three hundred pages is an intimidating task. That oh-so-long *middle* often causes authors to give up and stow the manuscript in a drawer. I hear you gulping.

Soooo, just how many unfinished novels *do* you have in that drawer? Do you take them out now and then to see if some kind literary fairy finished them for you? Or a cyber alien infused you with new ideas?

Whatever the genre, your plot must follow a predictable curve of escalating difficulty (complications) for both the protagonist and antagonist. These obstacles *must* intensify until your climax, which obviously needs to be the most suspenseful, emotional, or active scene in the book. It should answer questions the reader's been dying to know from the outset. This escalating series of complications don't have to be knock-down drag out battles, but must present the character(s) with increasing hardships in the journey toward their goal, whether it be joining with a lifemate or preventing the destruction of the universe.

After the climactic curve, the suspense, as such, drops in intensity while you wrap up the story.

If you're not sure about your story's escalating difficulties, try this: on separate index cards, list events that occur in each major scene. This might be by chapter; it might be by scenes within chapters. Lay the cards on your desk or tape them to the wall in order of occurrence.

Now stand back and really evaluate things. Do the events grow in importance, suspense and/or danger? Would changing the order of some make things smoother or more powerful?

As I write, I maintain a separate file that lists the important events within each chapter. Just a couple of sentences that keep things fresh in my mind: John killed Mary, Sarah found a letter from Gary.

This simplifies the final evaluation of the climactic curve. It also makes writing the synopsis easier (especially if you're required to do a chapter-by-chapter wrap-up) and, in the case of a mystery, you can see at a glance where you've left clues or red herrings. Color coding these helps—perhaps red type for clues, green for red herrings, blue for protagonist's problems and purple for the antagonist's conflicts.

By using the index cards, you'll also be able to see whether two chapters accomplish essentially the same goal. Sometimes this happens if you're writing in multiple viewpoints. If so, decide which scene is stronger, develops the best character, or does the most to forward the plot—then consider deleting one, or consolidating them.

Here is a collection of nitpicky but oh-so-important things that weren't long enough to warrant their own chapters.

• Is your opening sentence compelling? Does it interest the reader in what's going to happen next? You often see contests for the best FIRST LINE, or BEST OPENING PAGE. There's a reason for this, and it's not just to have another reason for a contest.

Great openings draw in the reader—insert adverb here…*immediately, quickly, compellingly*. Picture the shelf in the bookstore. A woman picks up your novel. Opens the cover. Thumbs past the title page and dedication. She reads a line. She closes the book and picks up someone else's.

Deflation buckles your knees.

Statistics say you have about thirty seconds to capture a potential reader's interest. That's essentially two paragraphs.

Think of some amazing first sentences that have been made popular through the years.

Call me Ishmael.

Lolita, light of my life, fire of my loins.

I am an invisible man.

You don't know about me without you have read a book by the name of The Adventures of Tom Sawyer; but that ain't no matter.

He was an old man who fished alone in a skiff in the Gulf Stream and he had gone eighty-four days now without taking a fish.

It was a pleasure to burn.

The cold passed reluctantly from the earth, and the retiring fogs revealed an army stretched out on the hills, resting.

If you don't recognize at least some of them, shame on you.

Question: wouldn't you love one of your openings to join these classics?

Don't tell anyone, but I'm about to reveal my most embarrassing moment. A few years ago I was at a workshop given by a well-known NY agent. It was an intensive workshop for authors who'd completed a manuscript—but not yet published.

As one of the final exercises of the weekend, he asked each of us to stand and read our opening sentence. That was it—just one sentence. He said for the rest of us to raise our hands if the line was compelling, if it made us want to hear more of the story.

I grew excited; I had a terrific opening line. I stood up and read the sentence so all could hear. *Paige couldn't believe Stefano would say such things.* Of the thirty people in the room, one hand went up...halfway. I wanted to crawl under the table.

I didn't, but the event etched itself in my mind. I went home and rewrote the opening. (Actually, based on that workshop I rewrote the entire novel)

FYI, the new first line of that novel: *If Paige Carmichael hadn't been standing in the doorway of Stefano's office, she probably wouldn't have heard the sound of the gunshot in the huge rambling mansion.* Hopefully all your hands are raised. Because of that exercise I now strive to make every chapter opening *and* closing as riveting as possible.

• I won't go into a lot of detail about point of view. It's a topic that can, and has, filled entire books, but there is one important thing to remember: do not switch points of view just because you feel like it, or because you like a particular character. If you like him that much, write another book with him as your main character.

Switch perspectives only when there's something your main point of view character *cannot* show the reader. Never switch in the middle of a scene and particularly not within a paragraph or, heaven forbid, within a sentence. "Yes," you argue, "I see books where it happens all the time."

Yes, it happens, especially in the older classics, but point of view is difficult for a beginning writer to do properly. A change from one character's perspective to another must be seamless, practically undetectable.

Another reason to use as few perspectives as possible—and this is a big reason—many publishers won't contract a book with too many. I work for one house in particular that, in their romances, they will only allow two points of view—that of the hero and the heroine. I can't tell you how many stories I've had to reject because there were more than those two. Think about it though, the story is about the relationship between those two people. It's not about the other characters.

As you go over your story, watch for things that aren't quite right, things that aren't *exactly* what your character is seeing or hearing or feeling. And don't be cagey about it. If the character's seeing or hearing doesn't happen easily, write so that it does. You are in control of the words on the pages. You have the power!

• Introduce characters slowly. Construct the story at the outset so you're not introducing too many characters at once. Two, or maybe three is all you should burden the reader with at the same time, especially in those opening scenes. More and the brain scrambles to keep them straight.

Also, when several people are in a group, try writing so only two, or maybe three, are talking at the same time.

• Do your verbs convey the exact tension, emotion, sadness, etc. that you want? Example: The hairs on the back of her neck stood on end as the scent of ammonia wafted along the breeze to taunt her nostrils. This isn't right because the scent of ammonia doesn't *waft* or *taunt*, it *erupts* and *stings*.

A big fault I see in novels I edit is the author who uses the same old verbs throughout the story, walked, turned, looked. Dig, invent, formulate...rewrite. You are the sole creator of this story. Make it the best it can be!

• Over a span of three or four hundred pages, it's easy to repeat words and descriptions. These repetitions are better detected if we read passages out loud. Reading aloud also reveals discrepancies in sentence rhythm, duplication of thought, unnatural dialogue, and overused sensory images. Reading out loud feels silly at first. Your dog will lift his head and wonder what the heck you're doing. Just remind him he does a lot of things you don't understand either, like licking his plumbing. Also, it's best to read to someone (not the dog) who has a copy of the manuscript. The reason, our brain tends to read things as they should be and will often skip over mistakes. A partner will spot the discrepancies.

Do you repeat the same phrases? One of my authors, in love scenes, repeated the word 'moved'. *He moved from one breast to the other. Then he moved lower. Then he moved back up.* Yes, it creates a visual image, but it's dull. Beef it up. Perhaps his fingers feather along her silken flesh. Or his lips caress her cheek. Close your eyes and get inside the character's head. Exactly what is he feeling (and please don't use the word *feel*)? What is he tasting, touching, smelling? What is he *doing*?

Is the same word repeated too closely together? More than once in a sentence? Or in a couple of sentences in the same paragraph? Sometimes this is done for effect, to accentuate a meaning. This method is called *conduplicatio*. Most times, when I see repetition, it's not *conduplicatio*, it's—sorry to say—laziness. (Or a person who hasn't read the story over and over and over.) Done by an author who lacks the self-assurance to go beyond what's familiar. Sometimes it's...cough... rush to get the story done and submitted. Remember time and distance?

Do you repeat character descriptions? For example, do you keep mentioning Sally's long blonde hair or Sam's sensuous golden eyes? If you've given a vivid and memorable description of Sally at the beginning—trust the reader to remember. When Sally flings that hair over her should the reader will be seeing blonde sparks flying. If you've shown Sam to best advantage, when he gazes at Louise on page 75, the reader's hormones will be a'twitchin'. Devise other ways to describe Sally's hair or Sam's eyes. OR better yet, leave it out completely. Trust the reader remember by himself.

• Do your descriptions of someone's physical appearance, the setting, clothing, or weather come in the middle of an action scene? If so, chances are it slows the action. If the setting is important, introduce it at the outset, while things are still calm. Or, the character can notice when things calm down. Perhaps she can contrast the mood created by the setting against what just transpired. If she's been there before she can think, wow, I'll never see this place in the same way again.

Recall the woman being mugged on that sidewalk. Will she ever pass that spot again without remembering?

This is a book about editing—things done *after* the draft is complete. But for a moment, let's talk about basic things. Things that should've been considered before, or during the writing.

• The plot must be believable, logical, and it goes without saying... interesting. A plot is a sequence of events connected in a cause-and-effect manner. Generally the plot consists of a series of increasingly more intense conflicts, a climax (the most intense part of the story), and a final resolution. The plot must be advanced as the story unfolds. We talked a bit about this in a previous chapter. But there are other considerations.

First, is your plot bold and fresh with distinctive and fun settings, or are there numerous scenes where the characters sit around drinking coffee or tapping out musical beats on their steering wheel?

Get the characters out of the house, car or shower. Bring in outside elements: weather, strangers, unique settings, other events related to your subplots. (Subplots? What are those? More later, grin.) Encourage those outside elements to stimulate new thoughts, images, conflicts, or scenes. Think how much more interesting events can be if the character(s) are affected by the fog rolling in over a mountain lake. Or the possibility that someone in the workday crowd overheard the murder plot. Or a traffic pileup makes the character late for a meeting to sign a pre-nup agreement. Ask yourself what moods or reactions those alternative settings can evoke within your story.

• Do you have a lot of scenes in coffee shops, restaurants, bars or other eating/drinking establishments? Unless a bomb goes off under Zack's chair, or a snake slithers from inside Charlotte's handbag, these are like shower scenes—BO-ring. And waaaay overused. In the manuscripts that cross my desk, at least half of them open with the characters meeting in some sort of eating or drinking place.

• What do your characters do for a living? When imagining the plot, did you fall back on familiar things like schoolteachers, waitresses, or writers? Sorry, but these are dull. Ordinary. Uninventive.

How much more unique can an astronaut or racecar driver or long distance runner make the plot? I hear you crying, "But I don't know anything about those careers."

Exactly my point.

It means research. It means taking longer to complete the manuscript, but the special-ness of the plot will give you a new perspective. It will open you up to a myriad of new sales markets, and publishing opportunities. I reject manuscripts all the time for the simple reason that they are ordinary.

How can you prevent a plot from being ordinary?

One way is to play the *what if* game. Let's say Yolanda meets up with Barry in the park. How do you bring this otherwise commonplace scene to life for the reader? How do you keep the characters moving in a forward motion?

Try listing seven things that can happen while they are in this park.

1-children are playing kickball. They invite Barry and Yolanda to play too

2-they're invaded by a swarm of red ants

3-Barry spills a glass of wine on Yolanda's white shorts

4-Yolanda's cell phone rings. It's work

5-Gerry arrives. He was once Yolanda's lover

6-Harry arrives. He was once Barry's lover

7-a pit bull runs up growling and snapping

The thing I recommend to my authors is to work backwards. Start with item number 7. See if you can work it into your scene. Why number 7 first? Because it's the least ordinary. It's the thing that was the hardest for you to think of.

The *what if* game can be done in any scene, under any circumstances. Trust me—if you employ it, you will have much more varied and compelling plots and subplots. What are subplots?

• Subplots are smaller stories within your story. Though they appear to be less prominent, less important, it's great fun to tie them into the main plot at your climax. How terrific when, as the main character uncovers a plot to overthrow the government, his teenage daughter is falling in with criminals who're perpetrating the overthrow.

Or, as your bank teller discovers the love of her life—her boss—he's framing her for embezzlement.

Sound doable? Fun?

More like scary and insurmountable, right?

No. But it takes planning.

Let's add another subplot to each of the plot ideas above. How about, as the main character uncovers a plot to overthrow the government and his teenage daughter is falling in with criminals who're perpetrating the overthrow—the next-door neighbor, who is an undercover CIA agent, sends in an operative to *distract* the daughter.

Or...as the bank teller finds the love of her life, and her boss frames her for embezzlement— her mother, to *save* the wayward daughter, begins dating that boss.

Devise your subplots so they can intersect in some way at the end of the book. Two ways to do this: work in alternating chapters where the subplots are seemingly unrelated, and bring them together at the end.

Another way is to let the reader in on every event as it's happening. They will form opinions as to how things will come out.

Either way, let the climactic sparks fly!

• Conflict. A story, a scene, and even a paragraph, isn't complete without conflict of some kind. Without a problem to solve, an obstacle to circumnavigate, a bomb to diffuse, there is no plot. No story. The conflict doesn't have to be earth-shattering. It can be as simple as a telephone ringing while the character is in the cooking dinner—she is conflicted about whether to answer. Doesn't matter what the conflict is. Make it something to mix up the status quo, so the character must re-think, alter a plan, change an event.

• Theme. What is the point of your story? Why should readers read your book, care about it, tell his friends, buy it for their mother?

Wikipedia describes theme as: a message…usually about life, society, or human nature.

Themes often explore timeless and universal ideas. Most themes are implied rather than explicitly stated. A theme might be overcoming adversity. Another might be growing old gracefully. Finding love after abuse.

Timeworn but effective: good vs. evil.

Some stories contain several themes. Most genred novels don't attempt to convey a message. But why not work something into your original plan? Think how much stronger the story could be. How much more poignant. Or saleable.

• As you write your synopsis (because you *will* need one), try also making a chapter by chapter outline. This doesn't have to be anything major. Doesn't even have to have complete sentences. Just a few words on what happens in the chapter. Many authors have adamantly told me they don't use outlines when they write. That's okay, this exercise isn't for the purpose of constructing the story. It's to determine the flow.

Does something pivotal to the plot happen in *every single* chapter? Complications drive the story forward. Your heroine escapes marauding raiders, only to find herself trapped in a dungeon with thousands of venomous snakes. She outruns the snakes and crashes headlong into a tsunami.

For plot twists and action, throw hurdles in your protagonist's path. These complications can be caused by a villain, opposing forces, natural causes, or even poor choices. They will not only propel the story's motion, but develop and strengthen your characters. You will learn things about him/her you didn't know at the beginning. The *what if* game is particularly helpful in devising plot twists.

An unfortunate side effect might be that you may have to go back and rewrite early chapters to incorporate the new personality traits. But again, we're talking strength of story. Completeness. Memorability.

Alone at Last

Okay. Feeling confident?

Here are some to try on your own. Whittle them down, beef them up, tweak to your heart's content. There's no exactly right or wrong answer.

❧ "I told you how the journal fell to the floor when I put my gear on the shelf. And about the loose paper I put back. I can't read German, but I did glance at it and saw what might have been a letter. Glenna's words at the grave reminded me she could speak French. After, we finished eating I asked her if she could read German as well. She said she could, sort of. So I showed her the paper in the journal. She only knew some of the words, but said it looked like a hand-written will. And something I'd missed. There was a deed to the property in an envelope in the back of the journal. Connie returned this to me and I replaced it on the shelf in the bedroom. As for the paper, I know a German lawyer in Chicago and will send that on to him." *Hint: There's some overwriting happening here.*

❧ "No, we're going now." Lester didn't wait for a response or any debate. He knew, like all women, Renee wouldn't be caught outside without fresh makeup, but he wasn't going to wait for that, not this time. He picked her up, nightgown and all, and quickly moved toward the front door. "Renee, hold my neck," and as she did, he grabbed the keys on the TV. Lester opened the door calmly, reached the car in four strides, and squealed hastily out of the driveway, not concerned with closing up before he left. *Hint: the same here, overwriting, with adverbs.*

●◆ At home, Sam went directly to the bedroom. He was exhausted. He removed his shirt, sniffed to see if any residual odor was left, and decided the clothes he was wearing could pass for another day. He placed the clothes on a hook in his closet. He grinned when he felt the note Lee clipped to the inside of the shirt pocket. "Better leave it there," he warned himself, otherwise he might forget to pick up the stuff she needed. *Hint: work on overwriting and pronouns here.*

●◆ "It seemed strange to me too. Frank sounded a bit upset, said he would tell us when we got here. He asked us to meet him at his house at nine. We used the code he gave me to get through the gate, and then rang the doorbell. When no one answered after two rings, I decided to leave a note. When I tried to stick it on the door, the door opened." Adam pointed at the sticky note still stuck on the front door. *Hint? Nope, you're getting too dependent—you're on your own.*

•❖ Clusters of mature trees sporadically dotted the community, declaring their permanent duty to both shade and beautify. By early October the majestic autumn foliage would create homage to Mother Nature like none other. Distinctively different and impeccably manicured landscaping flaunted the gas-lit parkway and all of the manors throughout the cul-de-sac in the pristine village known as Van Der Mere Estates. Dentists and lawyers, surgeons and newspapermen claimed the prestigious zip code as their home.

•❖ Wearing a tweed serge suit and silk shirt, a punctual Harry appeared at her door. He held out his arm for Jessica to grab. Masculine smelling cologne filled her aura. He drove a small, sporty car with a name Jessica had neither heard of nor could pronounce. He opened all doors, tipped the maitre 'd, pulled the chair out for her to sit and began a series of appreciative compliments.

•❖ The best compliment he could give Freda was to say she was average. He, on the other hand, was a symbol of the All-American athlete. Hanging a combination of twelve Degrees and Certificates on his office wall gave him the

Boston notoriety of "Businessman of the Year" award.   He was featured in the Boston Businessman Magazine and was guest of honor at the Carson Country Club. Two years ago he deliberately created an argument with *the help* labeling her too insufficient to be of Country Club membership. He went solo to the banquet and made it known to all that his wife had taken ill.

❧ "Phthe, twth." Nan spit what felt like yesterday's dried-out leftovers from her mouth. "Ohhh." She rolled over to a pile of leaves on the ground and a canopy of trees with leafy limbs that allowed tiny flickers of sunlight to filter through. It made her head hurt. The rich, earthy scent of forest moss, not unlike from when her father took the family hiking when she was a kid, was heavy in the air. "Where the heck...what the hell? Kenny? Kenny where are you?" Damn, it felt like she'd crashed again. Nan hissed while cracking open one eye. She hoped that despite the clean woody scent and soft, moist texture that felt like grass coupled with the crunch of dried leaves in her fingers was just an after affect of the crash. After all, the hospital told her that while she seemed totally okay after the crash, post traumatic stress could pop up at the most odd ball of times. Clearly the dream she had about being on the moon with that nuisance neighbor Sal posing as Adonis was just a symptom of that. Right? Right.

◦ "Okay, okay," Wendy said soothingly, feeling instantly guilty that she had considered not stopping. Subconsciously an internal switch flipped to ER nurse mode and Wendy sprung into action. "I'll call an ambulance for you." Quickly she dialed 911 and filled the dispatcher in on the situation. Stepping from the car she snatched the stethoscope off the seat and handed her cell phone to the distraught boyfriend. "What's your name?"

◦ Becoming pregnant was a condition Tina imposed upon herself. Clockwork had her touching her stomach with heightening anticipation. When Tina turned thirty-five she and husband, Victor, consulted a specialist who expertly stated teenagers and pre-menopausal women were among the most fertile candidates to conceive. Since Tina was neither, she took the doctor's advice, quit her lobbyist job at the bloodbank and began a regimen of daily fertility shots.

◦ Everything was real. Eleanor was in Atlanta 1863 in the midst of the Civil War's Confederate south. Tears welled once again and she lacked the strength to stem the onslaught that scorched her cheeks. Utterly dejected, she grasped at the thought this could be the chance for a new life she'd wanted, finding the surreal sense of peace just beyond reach. This morning memories of all it would mean to give up assaulted her brain. She could not reflexively reach for her cell phone, press speed dial number one, and call her mom. She could not watch the local news at the end of the day or sip a mojito to relax. In this time she would not even be allowed to vote. All of the rights women had gained in her time would be gone.

How Barb got through the next few minutes she had no idea. When that gate opened, she could be facing her father. Should she rush forward and hug him, or should she appear cool and introduce herself properly? She wondered how he'd react, finally coming face to face with his daughter after all these years. A dozen thoughts flew through her head. Would he recognize her? Would he be dark, tall? He was sure to be handsome, she thought.

Once they finished reading the letter Dixie had sighed in relief. He, on the other hand, was worried. She had missed the words in the letter *I saw the two of you together*. He started to feel like they were being stalked. The perpetrator of these letters had watched them for some time. The question was for how long? But whoever this was had seen them together. Where? Why mention it now? He was beginning to think the person who sent these letters was just a little crazy. And maybe, just maybe, he should rethink keeping Dixie at his side. She had been right about one thing this had become a dangerous game. Especially now with two men they hadn't known existed before thrown into the mix. Dixie may not be entirely innocent in this sordid game being played out, but that didn't mean she couldn't become a target like he obviously was. He knew he had to think seriously of separating from her until this informant decided to show his face.

The heat was beginning to soar; Ira wondered how he would endure another day with the sun blazing down upon him. Finding it difficult to breathe, the intense humidity smothering, he leaned back, absorbing the silky lull from the wind, as it blew gently from the northwest, rocking the boat up and down over the waves. Focusing on the continuous sway of the dinghy Ira listened to the rhythmic lap of the water as it slapped against the sides, attempting to soothe him into a peaceful tranquil state. Time stood still, only the present fear, piercing deep, *hurry, hurry* was all he heard, knowing he still wasn't safe.

Little Ann's lips trembled and her jaw set before trying to lever herself the rest of the way. "He won't die today." The commitment and determination in her voice stunned Joe. Her head disappeared and the vehicle moved beneath him as she shifted inside. Very soon the motor shut down and a loud cheer went up from the crowd. Anger soon replaced relief as he thought about how close she came to going over the side of the bridge. Damned little fool!

❧ ☐The first floor of the place was one common room. A primitive existence, like it had stood here for centuries, long before the smoke damage, which was considerable. Rustic pewter punched lanterns hung from the rafters overhead. Three plank tables had been pushed to one side of the room. They appeared unharmed from fire damage. However, charred chairs were scattered everywhere. The monstrous stone fireplace was also charred black. The fire which burned in its gaping hearth made the room cozy, nevertheless.

Here are a few plot ideas. See if you can expand subplots from them.

❧ ☐A man just released from prison, determined to turn his life around, he returns to a wife and two children. A parole officer makes most of her income blackmailing clients into robbing jewelry stores.

➽ ☐A librarian gives her illegitimate son up at birth. He grows into a terrible human being who taunts and cheats his fellow townspeople.

➽ A woman abused since childhood, hates men. One man becomes determined to change her mind.

About the Author

Cindy Davis is a recent transplant to south Florida. She enjoys the outdoors, whether hiking, camping, gardening or bringing the computer to the swing in the herb garden.

She is recently married to Rick—whom she met on Match.com. They are living proof that online dating can work. They even wrote a book about their individual experiences. Check it out: *Solving the Mystery of Online Dating; Finding Love and Relationships while Avoiding Scammers*.

Cindy has been a freelance editor for twenty-two years. She's had the pleasure of working with eight different publishing houses and more than five hundred authors on thousands of manuscripts. Many of her authors have gone on to find agents and big publishing contracts. www.fiction-doctor.com

Cindy is a multi-published author. She pens mostly mystery and romantic suspense but has recently branched out into New Age fiction. Check her out at www.cindydavisauthor.com.

If You Fall off the Horse, Dating After Divorce, co-authored with her husband Rick Palmacci

But Honey He has Purple Hair, Raising Kids with Sarcasm, Humor & Grit, co-authored with her husband Rick Palmacci

Make Money Breeding Small Dogs, co-authored with her husband Rick Palmacci

How to Resume Your Life, After the Death of a Spouse, co-authored with her husband Rick Palmacci

How I Lost a Thousand Pounds, Eating My Way to Better Health, Rick Palmacci